Our
Family
Tree

George Lightcap and his fiancée, Juliana (Judy),
1947; future parents of the poet's spouse

Our Family Tree

and other myths

poems by Jean LeBlanc

SHANTI ARTS PUBLISHING
BRUNSWICK, MAINE

Our Family Tree and Other Myths

Published by Shanti Arts LLC

193 Hillside Road
Brunswick, Maine 04011

shantiarts.com

Designed by Shanti Arts Designs

Cover image— [top] Painting of a tree by J. Camille LeBlanc, the author's father; [bottom] Photograph of J. Camille LeBlanc and Sydne Grace LeBlanc, around 1960. Used with permission.

Printed in the United States of America

ISBN: 978-1-971191-08-9 (softcover)

Library of Congress Control Number: 20269356591

Again, for my George

[left] Achille LeBlanc, the poet's paternal grandfather, in his bakery, year unknown [right] Pearl Raatikainen, the poet's maternal grandmother, dressed for a day at the beach, Easter 1950

Contents

Acknowledgments

I wish to thank the editors of the following publications in which these poems first appeared:

Ekphrasis: "Love" and "Snow Woman Returns to Her Winter Home" (Fall/Winter 2010)

Exit 13 Magazine: "January Thaw" (2024) and "My Latest Elaborate Mind Trick to Try to Fall Asleep" (forthcoming)

Journal of Pedagogy, Pluralism, and Practice: "Liberation" (2014)

The Kerf: "The Braid" (2011)

Memoir(and): "Some Flemish Painters Walk Around My Grandmother's Yard" (2011)

The Moving Force Journal: "Frost Heaves" and "Sorrow" (Spring 2020)

Off Line: An Anthology of New Jersey Poets (South Mountain Poets, 2010): "Looking Out Not Exactly to Sea"

Paper Nautilus: "Because All of Life Is Third Grade" (2012)

Platform Review: "Our Family Tree and Other Myths" and "Wife of the Poet" (2025)

Resonance: "Bibeau in the Buttercups"; "Bibeau's Legacy"; and "Old Bibeau, His Heart on His Sleeve" (2025)

Watching the Perseids: The Backwaters Press Twentieth Anniversary Anthology: "After the Bread, Then, Cake" (2017)

A Note About These Poems

These poems are visitors from the ever-shifting borderlands
between memory and imagination. The voices channeled by
these lines cross back and forth from the vicinity of fact to the
more interesting (artistically speaking) realm of truth. Do not
look for clues about my family in these poems. Instead, find the
clues about your family, and ask yourself, "How did she know?"

Dancing Couple in a Praxinoscope

On a tabletop by candlelight they waltz.
You spin it like you would a top, only
it turns in place, on a stationary stand.
The center turns, a center of mirrors,
a series of mirrors that reflect any image
you can dream. Your most recent dream
comes to hesitant life, diffident animation.
Fast, slower, slower, slow. Imagine music.
One two three, one two three. Imagine
these silent partners, dream partners
who never tire, never let go. How they
dream of us, these whirling things,
wondering how the mirrors make us seem
so singular, so still, so flat, so unalive.

When You Were Switched at Birth

When you were switched at birth, you knew right away
you were in the wrong bassinette,
and no bed has felt right since.

When you were switched at birth, you ended up
with a family for whom it was second nature to use tools,
fix things, tie knots, build stuff.

Your switched-at-birth family loved
fried clams, pork chops, instant potatoes.

Ten years after being switched at birth, you asked to move
into the unheated room at the top of the house.
Your own room. Cold but alone, no longer lonely.

You wonder about the possibilities that were erased.
You understand it might not have been a bad thing,
being switched at birth.

Twentyish years on, some other family looks on in wonder
as their odd child removes a door from its hinges, planes
a corner so that it closes properly, rehangs, paints,
cleans the brush, puts everything away.
They have baked potatoes with dinner.

It's not that you didn't love your family.
You just always suspected you were all
in the not-quite-right place.

Changeling

Tell no one. To my husband and everyone else I said she was the child of an unfortunate cousin. Then we moved from Quebec to New England where no one knew us, and so it was assumed she was ours. Tell no one, including her. Everywhere we lived, my garden provided more than we could consume, so one more mouth mattered not. Back in Canada, I gave the surplus to the nuns. They said grace over my Presbyterian squash. In return, they gave me her.

She had a face that rested into sadness. She liked to follow me into the garden, and quickly learned how to pull a weed, roots and all. She was their kin, a weed herself. But this she could not know. Rested into sadness, with frown and heavy lids and sunken cheeks. I pulled her hair back into two tight braids, to try to lift her expression upwards.

Every plant has a Latin name, she told me. There's the name most people call it, and the name the botanists have agreed upon. Those are the ones I must learn, she'd say, turning back to her book. Their true names.

Achilles the Baker at Work

Not the occupation one would expect
of an aging warrior, especially one with
a bad ankle, but after all those years
of funeral pyres, the unleavened loaves
set to bake afterwards upon the coals,
all those glowing coals, so as not to waste
the warmth—the living must eat, after all—
not such a strange choice perhaps, the smell
accustomed to his nostrils, the good rich scent
as well as the singe around the edges, the sight
of Patroclus dead, then Hector, the dough
slammed and slammed against the workbench,
the mouth of the oven glowing all night,
the hobbled gait as he approaches to jab
at the embers, a young boy named Achille,
learning his trade, the day's stories
still fresh and rising in his mind.

After the Bread, Then, Cake

After the bread, then, cake for the boy
whose birthday it is, the smell of cake
mixing with the smell of bread, the sweet

with the yeast, batter mixed and dough kneaded
and *your father has such muscles*
the other boys say on summer afternoons when I

smoke a pipe outdoors in my shirtsleeves
he goes to bed so early the boys say, but
their mothers understand, the earlier the bread

the better, for bread that cools at dawn is bread
that flavors the day, or some such thing my father
taught me, which I will not teach my son

who one day picked up a pencil nub and drew
the row of trees along the river. We all watched
his hand, watched his hand become *tree* the way

my hands become *bread*, and I knew then
the baking stops with me. After the bread, then, cake,
cake for breakfast, a gift of new pencils, and then back

to the bakery, the housewives coming for the best bread,
bread that when you slice it you see bread,
not air where your money used to be.

Egg Tempera

A singular light for every surface,

from the dancers' legs in a Degas

to Wyeth's chalky hills. Saturated

in light. More than light. Precision—

what the light would find, what it would pass by.

Think about light. Grind

the pigments. Paint your lover's shoulders

in mercury, arsenic, lead. Or glance

out the studio window, then immortalize the hen

with her own yolk.

Two Poems Inspired by Ando Hiroshige's View of Mount Haruna Under the Snow

1. Snow Woman

All night I listen to the storm, how it rattles
the walls of this cabin. The roofbeams creak
beneath the weight of the snow. But they hold,
as do I. In the morning, I make new footprints
to the woodpile and back. My little house
is painted red, so I can find it, even when
snow-blind. Of course, I am not telling you
anything new. You have your small red house,
your world of white, your few short weeks
of spring, when something grows,
something young and fine and maybe even
strong, but mortal. Before gathering up
an armful of wood, I write that word
with my finger in the snow: "mortal."
What word would you choose? Are they not
the same word, what the raven writes with
its talons, what the owl writes, the tips
of its feathers barely brushing the ground?
We wait, in our small red houses, fires
burning for one more day, at the center.
The leopard's pawprint just outside the door.

2. Snow Woman Returns to Her Winter Home

I ruined all my clothes in the lowland heat.
I am exhausted from the night-long sting
of insects. Those that don't sting
won't shut up. *Moonlight moonlight moonlight*
they rasp, every August night. At last,
I can climb back to the only four walls
I need, my little cupboard, my little stove.
One window that does not need a curtain,

covered on the outside with frost.
On the long mountain path, I resent
the switchbacks. Let me cut straight up
through the brambles, I want to tell
the overly-considerate maker of trails.
Another bend in the way answers, no,
you will have all winter to cut straight lines
through the snow. Front door to woodpile.
Front door to frozen well. Front door
to the overlook, where the summer world
floats below, an insect's short-lived dream.

January Thaw

Fields become ponds. Shallow, with corn stubble
showing through. Deeper, a flock of geese as
tenants. The little stream finds new strength,

dislodges a boulder or two from the old dam.
The Flatbrook all up over its bank, a mirror
of woods and sky. A small crowd

at Buttermilk Falls, despite the challenge:
the bridge below Walpack closed for repairs,
the south end of Mountain Road gated,

and Struble too. The only way in more water
than dirt, puddles of indeterminate depth.
But the Falls! A narrow white cascade

tumbling over itself down the ridge.
Everyone here on this winter day
has seen it before, but having seen

we know to come back, especially
during thaw. Knowing it's worth the effort. Worth
the long way in. Certainly worth a little mud.

Miserable at the Museum

The walk here was too many city blocks.

The stairs are too steep, too many floors
of too-modern art.

Everything is angular and contrary. Nothing
offers a comforting narrative of the world
as I wish it.

The gift shop is crowded.

The price of a cup of tea in the cafe is absurd.

The one painting we hoped to see is out on loan.

It is too hot. The maps on the walls are confusing.

A child is crying. Who would bring a child
to see this?

The guards watch me, knowing I will do
something wrong. Do I look as if I would
pull out a knife and slash these things?
Perhaps I do.

Water and a tea bag should be free, for what we paid
to get in. Do they charge us to leave, as well?

The parking garage is this way.

No, it isn't.

Outside, rats with wings.

My Mother Leaves the Building

"We lost your mother," the director of the memory care facility
tells me, quickly adding that my mother is literally lost, escaped,
somewhere out there in the world.

A back-and-forth of calls, waves of worry and anger
until, an hour later, the local police find her, walking in town.
Tired. Confused, of course. But easily redirected,

the nurse assures me. It's one of their standard phrases:
"She is easily redirected." How she might have
escaped (not the word I should use, but it's the one

that always comes to mind): The elevator—
just out of sight of the nurses' station—opens.
She just happens to be standing there.

No one sees her step inside.
When it opens again, she's in the kitchen, empty
at that moment while the staff delivers meal trays

to other floors. She finds the unlocked door
to the side parking lot. Like a bird, whose cage . . .
Like any one of us, looking for home.

Escape

She is naked, having shed her own diaper, pulled off her
socks. Everyone's back is turned to small tasks, no eyes on her
just long enough. Front door open to the light. A small step
over the threshold. Bliss of sun on skin! A few more steps
into this ecstasy, chubby arms reaching to the sky. But the
unpleasantness of soles meeting sharp and gritty makes her stop,
look down. A scream from within—good-bye to sun, to the bad
floor and its unforgiving otherness. Even without words, she
knows this journey must be repeated. Next time, with socks.

untitled

I watch for my mother to arrive. She is driving
from Massachusetts to New Jersey to visit us,
my husband and me. She is not a confident driver
(I inherited that from her), but here she is,
a little shaky, smiling a proud martyr's smile.
We bring her indoors, make her sit ("But I've
been sitting for hours"). I hug her, her slight frame,
bony shoulders not conducive to being hugged.
I ask about the trip. "I made it," is all the description
she has to offer. "I made it." How good it is to see her.
She looks so well, if a bit frail. I try to hold her, and
she turns into a bird in my hands, a warbler
or wren, trembling, nervous, a creature more at home
in secret places, green places, more at home
in memory, more at home where nothing
hugs or holds, except maybe shadows,
the pale green light, a final memory
having made it through the night.

Questions for Study

Throughout the novel, the main character
traces the outline of their hand. What is
the significance of this gesture?

What purpose is served by the flashback
to the parade on Main Street? Why
are the parking meters covered with little hoods?

Why does the main character dislike
store-bought roses? What do the roses symbolize?
What about the baby's breath?

What purpose is served by the flashback
to the family vacation, where the main character
tries to imagine pilgrims walking on their knees
up the stone steps to the cathedral?

Surely you do not think the cathedral is a symbol?
Or the pilgrims with bruised and bloody knees?
How many stone steps were there?

Did you even notice this novel was written
in an imaginary alphabet? Trace the outline
of your hand; fill the outline with imaginary letters.

Can you picture your mother, her back to the parade
and her face behind the camera, taking a picture of you?

Poor Joyce Kilmer

I encourage my students to laugh at your most (only) famous poem. I hold it up as an example of everything that modern poetry—good poetry of any time—isn't. Inane. Naive. Pathetic personification of a generic tree. God appears twice, a stand-in for the absence of anything profound. A revolting poem. Or is it an actual revolt against all that is dark, all that is death, all that would be unleashed the year following its publication, in the war to end all wars? An expression of the obtuseness that led to that war, to all wars. Made by fools, indeed—war, I mean, not poems—the great abyss of waste into which you yourself would fall, victim of a sniper's bullet. May I suggest, then, with a minor change in syntax, your new last line: "but God can only make a tree."

Vinny's Diary

—Do you dream in color, I ask E.
—Not color, exactly, but light. A dream begins with a little burst
  of sparks. Then in the dream I am suddenly aware of where I
  am. The garden, or the dormitory at school. There are no objects,
  exactly, only streaks and planes of light of various intensities.
  And I am light, a cool light, like the moon. If in the dream I walk,
  or move at all, everything around me, all the light, ripples. But
  somehow it seems perfectly natural to be light moving through
  light.

—the tips of my pink shoes my pink dress I am running—

—remember: to her, words are like birds—

—The same pair of catbirds come back to nest in the hedge every
  spring.
—How do you know they are the same ones?
—I've known them longer than I have known you.
  Who else has a sister who says such things?

Night Terrors

Go tell your little sister a story to help her sleep.

Many of her stories feature wildcats. Our tame hills weren't always
so tame, one story begins. Cat Swamp is named for the one that
would chase its prey onto thin ice, let the prey—deer or human—
decide its own demise. Shades of Death was infamous for all the
catamount attacks.

The lovely mountain laurel, which grows in thickets so dense its
twisting trunks and branches overlap and interlock and make
what's called laurel hell, is a perfect trap for a child to get lost in.
The wildcat's ears are especially attuned to the pitch of a crying
child. Dinner for her cubs.

And another story on the mountain laurel theme. A naughty
child craves something sweet, hides in the pantry and eats a
pot of honey with a spoon. But this honey was made from the
poisonous flowers of that plant. And who knows for certain
where our bees have been.

Her favorite trick is to assure me I'm adopted. Your real parents
were unlucky residents of Shades of Death. One hot summer,
miasma settled in over that swampy place. Everyone turned
yellow and died in their beds, except somehow you. Mother and
father took pity and brought you here to live with us, and aren't
we blessed. The end.

The Motorcycle in the Room

it cannot be in the middle of the living room
but you are only four or five years old
watching your oldest brother and your father
argue about a motorcycle

shouting over one another
the motorcycle right there between them

in the center of the room a motorcycle
tilting at rest on its kickstand

you've never heard voices raised quite like this
dissolving couch coffee table
in their place a conjuring

sixty years on the owners of those voices
long silenced you still see

that motorcycle in the room
and you know it is a trick of memory
but you also know you witnessed
the casting of a spell

a family forever circling around
the weight of all that isn't there

The Ocean's East

Pearl. A prophecy, right? A piece of grit that gets in there
somehow (the perils of living in sand), right where you don't
want it, so you do what you can to smooth it out. Pearl. Owned
best-in-show for her jams: red currant, gooseberry, blueberry,
raspberry, blackberry, pear. Would only enter her own Grange
fair; said it would just be showing off to go to all the others, win
there too. Let old Betty Sawyer think her store-bought peaches
are the cat's meow in Lunenburg, Serina Fisk and her sour
strawberries out in Templeton.

And our day trips to the ocean. Hampton Beach, Buzzards Bay,
Old Orchard if we're up and out early enough, before sunrise in
April—that's right, April on the beach, a wind that cuts through
layers. Striding through the sand, looking for a little warmth
up in the dunes. Bathing suits beneath wool jackets. Sunglasses,
mittens. Are you having fun, girls? Yes, we'd say through
chattering teeth. Yes, Ma. Thank you, Ma.

When I graduated from high school and got a full-time job, I
started calling her by her first name. How many daughters get
to call their mothers Pearl? The ocean's east, the beach is cold in
April, except if she asks, say Thank you, Ma, we're fine, we're fine.

Old Woman in the Garden

She has arthritis, back spasms—
just reaching for a tissue can bring pain—
so for her to pull weeds and lop a few
walnut saplings takes courage.

Someone with the strength of a goddess
is required to fight the bittersweet,
the bindweed, the snakeroot.
All the usual enemies.

"I'm just an old woman," she'd reply,
"and never was very strong. The world
is too full of narcissists. Let's not go
conjuring goddesses."

She passes over every third sapling,
won't see them until tomorrow
when she critiques her work.
The old woman in the garden

apologizes to the mint. Most of it
must go, too. It will come back.
There is so much to do.
So much that won't be done.

Some Flemish Painters Walk
Around My Grandmother's Yard

They admire the lines of the rusting swing set out by
the tall white pines. One of the painters remarks
that the pines are like five brothers, keeping watch,
faces always to the wind. But it is the fruit and flowers

in this yard that have brought them, the painters, here.
Isaac Soreau fills his arms with bunches of black-blue
grapes, walnuts bursting from their puckered husks—
he loves the sharp smell, does not mind that they stain

his hands—'Like paint!' he says, and heads off toward
the windfall apples, wants one bruised just so.
Jan Davidsz de Heem is nose-deep in the asters.
My grandmother clucks her tongue at them,

keeping them somewhat in line, but it's like
herding artists—stop one from pulling a bean vine
up by the roots, the other's plucking currants as if
he'd strip the bush of leaves. And indoors,

Willem Claesz Heda is painting a pie. A pie!
What are they thinking? my grandmother asks,
though she understands the pride of these things,
decades of Grange fairs, every farmer in the county

arranging mounds of golden squash, great purple eggplant,
gleaming carrots, all just so, for the judges' eyes,
all the *stilleven* and *landschap*, the quilts and jellies,
backyard abundance, and oh! The Flemish painters

in my grandmother's yard hear her say she has every
butterfly wing she's ever found, and they trip
over one another, running for her cupboards,
strewing abundance in their ruffled wake.

Liberation

—after Winslow Homer's painting Summer Night

I like to pretend that's my grandmother as a young woman,
that last figure on the left, silhouetted against the surf.
Pearl—Miss Booth she was—is on vacation

with her classmates from Fitchburg Normal School.
The full moon that rose at sunset is overhead by now,
but sleep is the last thing on their minds.

If dinner was at eight, perhaps this started as
an after-dinner stroll. However they came to be
on the edge of the sea past midnight, surely now

they are bewitched by the tidal swell. Five sit
on their rocky perch, while two free spirits,
overcome by the uncanny blue, waltz to the rhythm

of the breakers. The others see them, laugh,
and join the dance. My grandmother lets the other girls
partner up, while she enjoys a solo seaside swirl.

She was nine when Winslow Homer died,
so she could not be that woman on the beach.
It's the profile that makes me invent this truth,

the same profile my father sketched of Pearl
in her late sixties. And yet, you see her as clearly
as I can: a young woman, about to stand and lift her arms

above her head, quite pleased with a night so free
that she concedes a flash of modest ankle
to a magnanimous summer moon.

Every Day, A New Version

1

Memories of the Great War were still fresh, the year she finished Normal School and started teaching, met a man whose past was, he said, best left in the past. A soldier, she guessed, though for which side. His family still in his birth country, which, if she ever knew the name of, she could not find on any map. Family business called him back. Of course he promised to return. Of course she let herself believe.

2

"We didn't know we were between wars." That's all she says about that time. Not how he promised to return after seeing to unfinished business in his birth country (a place no longer named on any map). Was it "unfinished business" or "family business"—perhaps both. Did he know she was pregnant when he left. Probably "family business" was the phrase he used, to hide from her the risk. Anagram—the only trace of him in his daughter's name.

3

She asks me what I learned in school that day, and I describe the double helix, like a twisted ladder, and how our chromosomes come half from one parent, half from the other. She bends to check the muffins in the oven, her face turning red from the heat. All we learned that day, things we can't see affecting things we can see. We had no idea of any of that when I was in school, she says. No idea at all.

4

More and more regular folks had automobiles, but a small town was still a small town, and two towns away was enough distance that she could answer new neighbors' questions with "widow," and people didn't pry. Enough distance between "what a shame" and "shame."

5

Her own parents dead, too, even her stepfather, who had been their hired hand when her father had still been living. Mother and both husbands, three names sharing one stone.

6

On her own at fifteen. The war, then the flu pandemic. An orphan in a world of orphans. Every day, she tries out a new version of her own story.

Our Family Tree and Other Myths

Somewhere in these low-lying leaves,
a lie. Commission or omission. Shame
or kindness, siblings as they are.

What the genes reveal, the paper trail
goes nowhere near. Does it matter enough
that, if you could have the dead back

for an hour, these would be the questions
you would ask? Would you bring
mortification or misplaced kind intent

into the open, watch their faces
collapse from awe to anguish?
Interrogate them into silence—

why should the dead be any different
from the living, why shouldn't secrets
be the fruits that never fall?

Hearth and Home

After a few months the questions mostly stopped.
The neighbors returned to their own affairs. Soon
there were questions of more pressing concern:

Would you see fit to take these eggs in exchange
for two or three squash from your garden?
(She'd give them five.) Two jars of jam

and a loaf of homemade bread for a few
good linen hankies, They were my mother's . . .
(She'd embroider the edges and give them back

to that neighbor's daughter, newly engaged.)
And not just food: a bouquet of gladiolas
for that same girl's parlor wedding.

Her garden and berry patch helped them all
through the Depression, then the war years too.
By then her own daughter was married,

though she knew that wouldn't last,
that she'd come home. Her daughter no good
in garden or in kitchen, lacked

the touch for both, but she could type
and do the shorthand, and she found work
in town. Then the town gave them money

to take a piece of land for a playground, a ballfield.
She planted wisteria, iris, roses. Fed the birds.
Hung a painting done by her daughter's new husband

over the fireplace, where she'd learned to make a roux
to thicken soups to stews that first long winter,
a two-room house and one dutch oven hers, all hers.

Old Bibeau, His Heart on His Sleeve

Old Bibeau, his heart on his sleeve, wheels for legs, a drop on
his nose, sings to the rabbits that visit the garden, the garden
as it once was known. Sings to them from the porch where, in
June, the longest days, he stretches his arms out in the sun. In the
garden as it once was known, volunteer morning glories climb
everything. At least that's what he thinks he sees, those few blue
dots. And if I am imagining it, sings old Bibeau, so what? Isn't
imagining seeing too? The rabbit chews a plantain leaf, loves
the weeds, as does old Bibeau. He would sing to the weeds if he
thought they needed song. Grow, grow, this world is yours, sings
old Bibeau, to rabbits, to vines, to grasses, to the occasional iris
that bursts through it all, one purple heart-shaped heart-sized
flower. It brings a tear to the cheek of old Bibeau, seeing it all, so
many songs to sing.

Bibeau in the Buttercups

No one believes Old Bibeau's story of being in buttercups up to
his knees. No one thinks to imagine Old Bibeau as bébé Bibeau,
just learning to walk, allowed to wander off the picnic blanket
and onto the lawn, the first warm day of spring, buttercups
brushing chubby legs, "a t'ounsand buttercup," chants Old
Bibeau long after everyone has stopped listening. It's true the
idea of "thousands" is an overlay of memories, decades of that
corner of the yard untouched by blade, left to become meadow.
But you doubt Old Bibeau at your peril, your own imagination
revealing itself as some withered unloved winter thing.

Bibeau's Estate

At first they dismiss the fantastical images, make-believe floral
hallucinations, until they realize this is Bibeau's sketchbook
from boyhood explorations of peat bogs deep in the north
woods, far from the truant officers who knew him by name.
Pitcher plant, sundew, orchid or lily, muddy thumbprints on
the edges of a few pages, and a landscape/self-portrait of bog
ringed by spruce, Bibeau's one foot bare and one in its boot in
the foreground, testament of a misstep on the floating mat that
sucked off boot and sock and might have held young Bibeau
fast forever, if not for his strength even as a boy, "Bibeau Bibeau
built like a bus" as his schoolmates used to sing. Bibeau's bog,
under Bibeau's sky, in the spring of Bibeau's life, all in Bibeau's
own hand.

It's an Heirloom

"His descendants still have the two-seated rocker that
he used as a driving seat." —William C. Armstrong,
Pioneer Families of Northwestern New Jersey

Old English *geloma*, a tool, becomes *ayre lome*
in Middle English, an implement inseparable
from the property itself, not just a weaver's loom
but all tools of all trades. Another century or two,

and an heirloom is anything one generation leaves
to the next, even brick-a-brack the young learn
to separate into donate, recycle, discard.
Genealogists aver that such possessions reveal

so much about an ancestor. Not only letters or diaries,
but a hoard of cake and muffin tins, or a dresser drawer
full of unused embroidered handkerchiefs
has a story to tell. Some things do make the living pause:

his paintings, a few oil studies on scraps of boards
from the days he dreamed of art school, but knew
the money would be better put toward life
in a new country, perhaps English lessons.

Large landscapes of the land he left behind,
larger ones of lands he'd never seen,
impossible mountain peaks. One adult child
takes a seascape, almost familiar, perhaps

that spot we'd drive to in early spring, too cold
but no traffic or crowds. But there are so many,
these paintings, some really not that good,
some losing flakes of paint in places.

Someone has a closet or a basement corner,
room enough to keep a few heirlooms no one
really wants but no one wants to be the one
to take to the landfill, make that final letting go.

Sorrow

I am the table, polished, smooth, reflecting sky.
I am the rocker, always promising repose.
I am the blue-white walls and blue-gray shadows

of your favorite corner. I am the curtains.
If you want, I'll be the wind that billows them,
I'll be the stillness between gusts.

I am the window; I am the distance that it frames.
The orange roofs over all those other lives.
The road to the blue hills.

I am the flowers in the vase,
sentinel and still, seeing what may happen
in all four corners of the room,

watching the road, the empty road.
Keeping secrets, even from each other.
I am the vase, who knows all,

knows when a petal is about to fall,
knows that when it falls, it will land on sky,
knows that the empty road is still a road.

I am the idea you have in the morning,
which, by evening, you know
you must let go. You must.

Ancestry-ish

Twenty generations back. Or two. Switched at birth. A turn of the foundling wheel. Angel-sent. Saved from the river. Kept by the wetnurse when the mother dies. Too many mouths already, the newborn offered to the barren neighbor. A niece or nephew raised as your own. Simply left by the side of the road, for a traveler with heart and means. Passed over by plague. Pulled from the rubble. Exposed. Adopted. Secrets gone to several graves. Hope for a chance. No hope at all. How did each of us end up with this life, this name. How did any of us.

The Philosopher's Daughter
Runs Away from Home

Beyond the front door, I live by my own logic. My father
considers himself the equal of Socrates and Christ, so I eschew
all streets whose names begin with "S" or "C." If I see a steeple
ahead, I turn the nearest corner. Try walking through this
sanctimonious city keeping all churches at your back—I'll solve
this puzzle, how not to walk in circles. My father walks and
talks in all-embracing circles. Somewhere there's a straight, wide
boulevard, sermon-free, just the trolley's bell alerting riders to
each stop, where I can out-pace parables, questions, paternal
scrutiny of the battle between defiant spirit and eternal soul.

The Philosopher Standing
at the Door of the Bank

Although it is an ordinary weekday, he has dressed in his Sunday
suit, least-frayed cuffs and collar, best funeral tie. He straightens
his spine to brace for the jargon of mortgage and debt. Perhaps
a fresh crew-cut before asking for a loan. The mechanism of
the walk-in safe—he imagines he can hear it from the sidewalk,
a persistent clicking and hissing of metal against metal. The
wealth of nations just on the other side of this wall— the small
figure on the street pulls at the single thread that holds the
button in place.

The Philosopher Goes with Fergus

Knowing himself to be an exiled king, our philosopher
retreats to the outskirts of a village surrounded by woods, a
village of other exiles, some of whom live even deeper in the
shadows and build or borrow what they need and live on beans.
Unencumbered by worldly goods, he hardly mourns the beloved
books gone under the auctioneer's hammer (our philosopher
did his best to learn them by heart). A bit disheveled, he uses his
waistcoat to carry home a cache of apples from some outlying
orchard. Apples sautéed with field greens for dinner, applesauce
for dessert. A meal fit for royalty, he tells the children. Children
grown thin on philosophy, on their own hopes and fears.

Courting on the Bridge of Flowers

At first, we scandalized the Shelburne Falls Women's Club
with our hand-holding and our whispers. The good ladies

blushed petunia-pink, or went all white like baby's breath,
those first few weeks. But it was spring; the whole world

was shy with newness, trying to hide its naked arms, its green
and supple thoughts. The ladies got used to us, even nodded

our way, as the world went full with summer. And still
the Bridge of Flowers bloomed, and still we held hands,

even talked of winter, just another cold glance we'd warm.
We talked of the river, and the old rail line that served the mills.

We talked of past as now, of future as assured. We talked of
bridges,
talked of time. All those perennial, given, undisputed things.

Yvonne 1905

A young woman skates on an unknown pond. Behind her, other
figures silhouetted against the snow-covered hill, silhouettes of
white pine and spruce. A farmhouse just over the rise, big house
with an ell and connected barn.

Distant cousin? Great great aunt? A photo taken by a friend, or
maybe a beau, so pleased with the Brownie camera he bought
with money saved from his job in his uncle's bakery, sweeping
flour from the floor and lighting cigarettes for the men in dough
up to their elbows.

She leans slightly to her right, skirt and arms caught mid-swing.
She looks directly at the camera, but everything's a little blurred,
her expression indistinct. The next moment she turns and glides
off across the ice, free.

Wife of the Poet

Look for my name in the index.
Look under "wife."
Look under "influences."
Look under last year's leaves, matted down
by months of snow, in the iris bed.

Look through boxes
of books, of papers
from that year of teaching
at a small private college.
Tea and cake, the devoted spouse.

Look under "marriage." Ah!
There you'll find the list of grievances:
Children, burden of.
Madness, family history of.
Money, problems with.

Although you could have found me,
once, at the edge of that iris bed,
cutting blooms that came
too early, a deceptive spring
here then not.

Or maybe in the meadow
where one year, indigo buntings—
but that's gone now, too,
the controlled burn,
the plowing under.

Walking Away

The day you say good-bye, I know exactly
what shoes you'll be wearing. I know
the pattern they'll make on the pavement,
after you walk down the wet stairs.
I know it will be raining. Your posture
will be impeccable, despite the rain.
I will look around for something
to fling at you, just to make you
flinch as it whizzes by your ear.
A book, I think I shall throw.
A paperback. But a thick one.
Of course, the book will open
as soon as it leaves my hand,
catch too much air, and not even
come close to your head. Your imperious
head! I hate you. The day you say
good-bye, I hope you ruin
your good shoes in the deep puddle
that collects at the end of the driveway.
I hope your wet feet bring on the sniffles,
the beginnings of a bunion, athlete's foot.
Something I can cure you of
when you come crawling back.

Frost Heaves

Not a country famous for its sunlight.
There's maple sugar season, the rising sap
diverted into buckets, boiled down
to crystal sweetness that cuts right through
your teeth. Two months later: apple blossoms,
if there isn't a late snow or hard freeze
(no one in these parts trusts early May).
Put up those memories well, the syrup
and the blush, and the other few fine days.
It's not much to live on, when that
peculiar gray returns. Night, cloud, silence—
we're beyond such quotidian terrain.
The soul's a small-windowed house
on a north-facing slope. Welcome home.

Ghost at the Table

—in memory of M. L.

The look in his eyes of someone who has committed
one of the two real sins: having wasted time by wishing it away.
A hole in him, where that time should be.
Working in the prison kitchen to fill the days,

to fall exhausted onto his cot and sleep despite the light
that always burns. Six months a blur of sameness,
one long day. The best part: taking garbage out to the bins,
looking up at sky. Any weather. Rain was especially nice.

After his release, standing barefoot in his sister's yard.
The pliant grass. Silent at dinner. The gleam of knife and fork.
A light switch always within reach. Only six months, they say.
You're here now. What more can they offer. The other sin?

Thwarting love. That played into it, too. She kept
his beloved cat, a Russian blue, those green eyes.
Not ghost, singular. Ghosts. Ghosts at this table. Ghosts
with knives and forks. Time on their hands.

My Latest Elaborate Mind Trick
to Try to Fall Asleep

It is 1850 or thereabouts. I must cook dinner, but what, and how.
Out behind the kitchen garden there's a summer stove
unconnected to the main house in case of fire. Good for
simmering

stews and soups, which can then steam dumplings.
Roasting squash when it comes in. The trick is carrying it all
back inside, cast iron pots along the uneven path.

Years will wear it smooth and level, I suppose.
Winters are an easier distance, biscuits and gravy
more often than not. And since this is a coastal town,

scallops browned with rosemary butter on a bed of greens
a nice quick dish. Elaborate fantasies for someone who hates
to cook, modern conveniences notwithstanding.

Years will wear it smooth and level, this path
where long skirts brush the chives and dill,
where rosehips beg to be pithed and steeped,

where flagstones, a century hence, will dip a little
in the center, smooth from countless footfalls.
Where at the end of it ghosts sit patiently at table,

napkins secured around spectral necks, admiring
the gleaming bowls of chowder, a feast untasted,
hunger the one real thing in this dream.

My Face Is to the Rising Sun

—title of a book published by the Whitman Publishing
Company, Racine, Wisconsin, 1931

Hardcover, but pocket-sized, when pockets
may have been the only place a person had
to keep a book, bookshelves long since
broken up for fuel, or sold, the house lost
to the bank, family scattered, no money for rent,
and perhaps nights by a railroad track outside
some small town, and the good people
at Whitman—oh to have a job!—know it is more than
a stale crust of bread someone threw out for
sparrows, more than a thin soup of twice-boiled
pigs' feet, that keeps a body going. Poetry!
The little volume opened in the firelight, and even
men who have never heard of Lord Byron,
who might scoff at his very name, will nod at this:
"He who surpasses or subdues mankind, must
look down on the hate of those below." Thank you,
kind people at Whitman, kind Racine, though the pages
go all brittle in the wind—you must cut corners too,
we know—thank you for *My Face Is to the Rising Sun*,
for "Be glad of rain," as world-renowned Anonymous
suggests. Most days, I am glad to have a face to turn
skyward, to live, like the birds, for free.

We Cut School, Take the Bus into the City

We make our way uptown to the museum, not to go inside,
but to buy a pretzel from the vendor as if he's the only
pretzel vendor in New York, and also to sit on those
great granite steps and suck the salt and toss a few crumbs
to the pigeons. This exact vendor, these precise birds, that
is why we cut school. The rest of the day, well, so what
if we are soon footsore, close to broke after two pretzels.
Somewhere, a pigeon coos to her chicks about generosity.
Somewhere, a pink face in a stroller loves us for handing her
the doll she had dropped. Somewhere, an older girl
breaks the cardinal rule and makes eye contact, and smiles,
and aren't we something, and for the next ten schooldays,
cityscapes fill our notebooks, detention after detention,
page after page of birds.

Time Traveler

A massive earthquake continents away shifts
the angle of our planet's axis, and along with it,
time. You look out your window

and there goes Emerson, his long strides
casting impossible shadows across the intersection
which is busy with carriages, men pulling carts

of vegetables, booksellers' kiosks, ladies in hats.
You could run after him—it is Emerson, no less!—
but something stops you, doubles you over

with grief. *Am I here alone*, you wonder,
am I the only one? What good to accost
poor Emerson in the street, tell him about

the years to come, be Emerson's private prophet,
if you cannot go home at night
and tell someone the news? *I said to him,*

You must adapt your Transcendental mind to
incorporate the less Romantic days to come,
the Shilohs, the assassins' bullets, the strife,

stay up all night revising, working it out,
so that one hundred fifty years from now
it won't all seem so quaint, so daft.

There goes Emerson, disappearing 'round the bend.
There you stand, dead with knowledge, wondering
why it should be impossible to recreate a world

already known, as if that slight shift of axis
shrugged off what was, good-byes never needed,
hellos never said.

What I Would Do to Be Hanged as a Witch

Give commands to my black cat
and be obeyed by this familiar.

Pass a neighbor's house
and will their dawn-breaking rooster dead.

Predict an eclipse, though I don't know
how real astronomers calculate such magic.

Passive things for a coward crone. Only the mildest conjuring
crosses my mind. This would have been enough

in central New England four centuries ago, helped along
by a nice outbreak of ergot in the grain.

But barn cats ignore me, intent on sleeping out their days,
bellies full of mice and chipmunks.

I keep looking towards the heavens, waiting for a shadow
to cross the sun. Waiting for the sound of a gallows

being built in the town square. Get to work, damn you,
carpenters, rope makers, thin-lipped parsons.

Smiling and nodding hello as I secretly covet their wives'
kitchen gardens, lace curtains, Sunday hats.

Death and the Miser

— painting by Hieronymus Bosch

And what great misers we all are, hoarding
anything easily within reach: books,
memories, photographs, money of course,
but also excuses, the lies we tell
ourselves—*I am happy, or why I'm not,*
and magical rise-and-shines that send us
out each day to ply our miserly trades,
count our miserly returns, and settle.
Our poets tell us Death is the mother
of beauty—Death, the expert miser,
gatherer of all, always, forever
never letting go, cosmic key keeper.
Our inspiration: Death. Our paragon.
Mini-miser, in Death's image: *hold on*.

The Obituary Writer

1

It was meant to be temporary, his first job after business school.
He had dreams of changing fields, oceanography, maybe geology.
In his small world he averaged ten obits a week, familiar names,
relatives of friends. As years went by, the friends themselves. A
week-long vacation each summer to a place where he could look
for fossils, or sit by the sea and marvel at the tides. The Bay of
Fundy made him weep with regret at never pursuing that degree.
His colleagues whispered that he looked somehow older after
that trip, wondered what had happened, never outright asked.

2

Ten or so obits a week. Familiar names, relatives of friends, the
friends themselves. Beloved spouse of. Surrounded by family. In
lieu of flowers.

3

For thirty years, ten or so obits a week. How many were polite
lies, how many complete fiction. An abusive parent transformed
into a saint. A double life, only half of which finds its way into
print. Offspring never acknowledged. You think you know
someone. You think you know yourself. The face in the mirror
reminds you, you know nothing.

Louisa May Alcott Reads
Barnaby Rudge to the Wounded

— Union Hotel Hospital, Washington, DC, 1862

There's this one nurse, Mother. She loves Mr. Dickens as much as
you. When I opened my eyes that first day here—three days after
the battle (during which I am certain the angel of death touched
my brow and said, "You are coming soon, son.") and the long
ride to this I guess one must call it a hospital—it was a moment
before I could discern I was alive, on a cot, and I heard her voice:

"Father Time is not always a hard parent, and, though he tarries
for none of his children, often lays his hand lightly upon those
who have used him well; making them old men and women
inexorably enough, but leaving their hearts and spirits young and
in full vigour."

And suddenly, Mother, her voice was yours, and your now-one-
armed farmboy is determined to outlive these stinks and screams
and see home again, though I cannot fathom how nor can I
promise when.

Lucy Say and *American Conchology*

Cholera comes to New Harmony. Long after dark, by candlelight,
I paint the engravings for my husband's books. Shell after shell,
page after page. I close my eyes for a moment and see the waves
come crashing, breakers before a storm, salt spray from the on-
shore breeze that drenches you even some good distance from
water's edge. Here in Indiana it's the river, slow packetboats that
sometimes bring the mail up from New Orleans, more often
bring the fevers, the fevered guests. Our good German prince,
shivering in our parlour, setting my husband Thomas aflame
with talk of every living thing that creeps upon this Earth.

There are freshwater shells, too, that tax my use of browns
and muddy greens. I pray for paper, ink, paint; pray our letters
arrive in Philadelphia; pray our packages survive the journey
back down the coast, through the gulf, up the Mississippi.
Wonder if our friends back east are still alive, or if a letter finds
them lost to us, months too late, undeliverable, or, if delivered,
causing only grief.

Thomas's eyes go yellow, his face hollow. This man who snatched
a beetle from the foot of a Kansa chief, who was declared a
medicine man on the spot, could use a little medicine himself.
The next boat may bring my new brushes, may bring news, may
bring books. Now I must paint.

The Botanist Edwin James

> "It enters my day dreams that I may yet go forth to gather weeds
> and stones and rubbish for the use of some who may value such
> things, and perhaps drop this life-wearied body beside some
> solitary stream in the wilderness."
> —Edwin James, in a letter to John Torrey, March 3, 1854

The steamboat, its leaky boiler. Barely enough power to go
against a current, limping upstream, nudging every shoal and
snag. And so we walked from the Mississippi River up across
the high plains and westward to the Rockies. I exaggerate, of
course, about the walking, but we did leave footprints in Eden,
geologizing, botanizing, Tom Say collecting his beetles with such
finesse the Indians declared him a medicine man. What a sight
we must have been, boys mucking in a slow stream, trying to
lure close a turtle that had a freshwater mussel clamped on each
flipper, to Tom's delight—five specimens in one, two phyla come
swimming to his arms, he laughed, the snapper lunging for the
bait. Then our happiness in discovering a leech on the reptile's
leg, a third phylum for our efforts in that stream.

As new as Adam, naming all we saw, a continent at our
feet. From the Great American Desert up into the Shining
Mountains, which we thought at first were clouds. No proper
bath in months, rough as trapper. Transported by a sky blue
mountain bell. The pains I took to fan the blossoms out so
that each one would be distinct within the press. In later
year, my colleagues would wonder why I never wrote about
the plants I collected on that journey, why I gave them all to
Torrey.

Having traveled all that way and back, I couldn't bring myself
to gaze upon the sheets within the press, the dried out leaves,
the flowers all gone brown and brittle. As if Adam had
thought to hold his breath when leaving Paradise, and, on the
other side, had exhaled, and tried to catch the outrushing air
in his suddenly unfamiliar, all-too-mortal hands.

Love

—after Jean François Millet's painting
Harvesters Resting (Ruth and Boaz)

As gold as ripe wheat in the sun, acres of it,
all that potential: the loaves, the loaves, the loaves,
and the rent will be paid, the beneficent landlord

made extra generous in this season of bounty.
And the rains hold off as the harvesters
gather armfuls of honeyed grass, bind the sheaves,

pile the sheaves into small mountains,
take their noontime rest on beds of the stuff,
so much wheat that some can be left – why not? –

for the gleaners. This is the world when we're in love.
But still we see the sickle blade glinting in the sun,
still our wary eyes lift skyward, each passing cloud

a sign to hurry, hurry – this luck can't hold forever.
And you begin to wonder, am I one
of the harvesters, do I belong?

Or am I the gleaner, Ruth the widow
in her robes of virgin blue?
All eyes turn to you: interloper, stranger.

Abundance down to this: one little life,
safe passage through the fields,
a few stray kernels tossed your way.

No. Let us be like Boaz, whose great heart
weathered true. Let us receive
what's left behind, and call it new.

The Braid

—photograph by John Strazza

How, by the end of the day, so many strands
from the nape down to the rubber band have
come loose. Better than loose—free. Dancers,
at opposite ends of the stage, twirling,
spinning, reaching, separate, yet so much more
than one. A great twisted yearning, a great
insistence on remaining loose. Free.
It is a mess, the woman would say, could
she see her own braid down her own back.
And yet, a lover would take the comb
from her hand, would say, *Let it be,
it is lovely*, and fingers would entwine
with hair, and shoulders would be kissed,
and then. Dancers. Reaching. Braid. No braid. Free.

My Imaginary Daughter

She's seven. She cartwheels
across the lawn, and ends
in laughter all elbows and knees.

She's ten. She beats me at chess,
shrugs as if it's nothing, this game
with funny pieces, a sluggish king and
capable queen who seem to have
no mutual affinity besides duty.

She's fourteen. She asks me to stop
writing poems about her, reminds me
that I hate other people's poems
about their children.

She's seventeen. She makes me walk a mile
every morning, color my hair,
wear sunglasses to avoid crow's feet,
stop wearing men's shirts out of the house,
pluck my eyebrows a little, especially
above my nose, and use mascara.

She's spending her junior year
in Paris. The house can't give her up.
The impression of her occupies
every chair. When I take a sweater
from my bureau, I find a long brown hair of hers
woven into the fibers. Late at night, a floorboard
creaks from the memory of her step.
A friend tells me, 'No matter how perfect they are,
they always leave you.' I've never seen this,
though: never seen a parent whose child
wasn't present, maybe just a furrow of the brow,
a heaviness of air, a fingerprint on
a little figurine, the whispered warning: 'Check.'

Because All of Life Is Third Grade

You'll never be the one who draws the best, no matter
how you love the arrangement of glass bottles the art teacher
has set up on her rolling cart. You just won't be able
to make the charcoal pencil in your hand echo those curves,
and you'll accidentally make what should be light, dark.

You'll never be quite as bad off as the boy who cries
at recess, on the playground.

You will sometimes have days when you are happily
staring out the window at the line of skinny trees,
and you'll angrily shake off the hand pushing
at your shoulder, and you'll turn to yell at the kid
who keeps pushing you, and it will turn out to be
the teacher, and no apology will suffice.

You will never finish that report on Brazil.

All photos of you will show your glasses slightly askew,
the part in your hair crooked, your goofy grin,
a button in the wrong buttonhole.

You will walk with Missy to the girls' room after lunch,
because she has diabetes and the teacher
doesn't want her to go alone, and you wonder
but do not ask, how she got it, when will it go away.

You'll just accept that it must be this way,
the glare of long hallways, the jostle of the bus,
the overnight exchange of best friends,
the sense of running as in a dream, every day
another page of fractions, another still life botched.

Looking Out Not Exactly to Sea

—after the photograph Man with Hat *by John Strazza*

Looking out not exactly to sea, but to harbor,
more city on the other side, not so distant,
a watery boulevard away, wondering where

river ends and estuary begins, and then
where the change from estuary to ocean,
knowing no such edges exist, that even now,

saltwater makes its way upstream, dense, deep,
persistent, carrying with it flattened specimens
of the life above, of flounder, of man with hat.

Two Full Moons in August

Summer moon, school moon.
Baseball moon, wait 'til next year moon.

Dusty green moon, birches have gone gold moon.
Dragonfly moon, warbler moon.

Last of the lilies moon, chrysanthemum moon.
In love with you moon, missing you moon.

Iced tea moon, hot cocoa moon.
State Fair moon, last big cookout moon.

Waves wash me to shore moon,
hawk over the lake moon.

Postcard moon, to do list moon.
Air conditioned moon, storm windows soon moon.

Wishing for a cold front moon,
hoping the hurricane turns out to sea moon.

Procrastinating moon.
Procrastinating moon.

Swallowtail moon. Monarch moon.
Sweet corn moon, apple pie moon.

Again I let the herbs go to seed moon,
even the mint is drooping moon.

Barefoot moon,
new shoes moon.

Make time stand still moon,
take us back moon.

JEAN LEBLANC grew up in Massachusetts midway between Henry David Thoreau and Emily Dickinson. After moving to northwestern New Jersey in 1994, she taught college writing and literature for twenty-five years. Her poetry appears in numerous journals and collections, including *Terrible Terrain: Poems Inspired by the Life of Lavinia Dickinson* (Shanti Arts, 2023). A vibrant local poetry community keeps her inspired, especially the Writers' Roundtable of Sussex County, New Jersey, and the Betty June Silconas Poetry Center, of which she is a past director. She also explores the transformative power of imagery using collage, asemic writing, and other visual media.

Shanti Arts

Nature • Art • Spirit

Please visit us online
to browse our entire book catalog,
including poetry collections and
non-fiction books on nature, healing,
art, and more.

Also take a look at our highly
regarded art and literary journal,
Still Point Arts Quarterly, a feast for
the eyes and the imagination —
available to download for free.

www.shantiarts.com

www.ingramcontent.com/pod-product-compliance
Lightning Source LLC
Chambersburg PA
CBHW021344060726
47591CB00006B/2150